I'm a Poet and Ya Know It Vol.1

Emilio J Montilla

Emilio J Montilla

DEDICATION

Este libro estas dedicado a mi mama Ana Soccorro Villaman. Gracias siempre por tu apollo en mis sueños. Gracias por mostrarme tu amor incondicional.
Te Adoro!

This book is for all those who were ever afraid to live beyond their fears, to actually allow themselves to dream and to pursue it despite their environment and lack of support from "friends" and family.

CONTENTS

1	Fallen Angels	Pg.1
2	Spoken Whispers	Pg.3
3	Cocktail Laughs	Pg.6
4	I've Created a Monster	Pg.8
5	Zombie Land	Pg.11
6	A Fine Ass Nerd	Pg.13
7	Butterscotch	Pg.15
8	Where's My Cape At?	Pg.17
9	Wait	Pg.20
10	Vanity	Pg.23
11	Meet Me in the Middle	Pg.26
12	Affectionate	Pg.28
13	My White T - Shirt	Pg.30
14	Floodgates	Pg.33
15	Settled	Pg.36
16	Chocolate	Pg.40
17	Desperation	Pg.43
18	Top of the Totem	Pg.45
19	Almost Famous	Pg.47
20	Vanity II	Pg.50
21	Candle	Pg.52
22	Got To	Pg.55
23	Clean	Pg.58

CONTENTS

24	Pity	Pg.61
25	The Rent Money	Pg.64
26	Hell	Pg.68
27	Slick	Pg.69
28	A Letter to Laziness	Pg.72
29	Ok with Uncomfortable	Pg.75
30	The Power of Language	Pg.77
31	Cloud of the Ghetto	Pg.79
32	Ignorance is Running This Bitch	Pg.81
33	Let the Bullshit Subside	Pg.84
34	I'm Platinum in the Shower	Pg.85
35	The Day I Found Out that Beautiful Women Farted	Pg.87
36	Alley – Oops	Pg.89
37	What Are Those?	Pg.93
38	Mind and Matter	Pg.95
39	It was Supposed to be Summertime	Pg.98
40	Hip Hop Stole My Tongue	Pg.100
41	New York	Pg,102
42	Let Them Know	Pg.105
43	To My Unborn	Pg.107

GLOSSARY

1	One Hitter Quitters	A one night stand	Fallen Angels (Line 9) P.1
2	Fender Benders	The doggy style sexual position	Fallen Angels (Line 9) P.1
3	Seed	A baby	Fallen Angels (Line 13) P.1
4	Monkey	Drug habit	Zombieland (Line 23) P.11
5	Prolly	Slang for the word probably	A Fine Ass Nerd (Line 5) P.13
6	Dope	Drugs/Cool	Butterscotch (Line 22) P.16
7	Respeck	The word respect by Music Producer Baby from Cash Money Records	Where's My Cape At? (Line 19) P.17
8	Vexed	Angry	Wait (Line 11) P.21
9	Pepe le pew ing	Stinking or smelling badly term used from Warner Bros. and Looney Tunes fictional character	Desperation (Line 3) P.43
10	The Show	Major League Baseball (MLB)	Desperation (Line 11) P.43
11	Pussy	Scared	Desperation (Line 13) P.44
12	Fanny	Butt cheeks	Vanity II (Line 22) P.50
13	The glove	A condom	Candle (Line 3) P.53
14	Swerve on	Having swagger	Clean (Line 27) P.59

		usually followed by walking with a limp	
15	Poured Up	Filling our cups to the top with alcohol	Clean (Line 8) P.59
16	Latest Steps	Brand new shoes	Clean (Line 14) P.59
17	Mean Mugs/Ice Grills	Angry, spiteful faces	Clean (Line 18,19) P.59
18	Hitting	Hitting the lotto or making it to the top of your goals and dreams.	Pity (Line 13) P.61
19	The Inevitable	Death	Pity (Line 21) P.62
20	CTC	Cut the check	The Rent Money (Line 17) P.65
21	Somama	Son of a bitch version from comedian Bernie Mac	The Rent Money (Line 16)P.66
22	Sucker Free	Honorable conduct, no slick sly or deceptiveness.	The Rent Money (Line 18) P.66
23	Wifed-up	Married	Slick (Line 7) P.69
24	Scratch Her Itch	Having sexual intercourse with her	Slick (Line 11) P.70
25	Eyes Fished	Looking, snooping around	Slick (Line 3) P.71
26	Bawdy	Body	The Day I Found Out Beautiful Women Farted (Line 1) P. 87
27	Hot Steppers	Dope or cool shoes	What Are Those? (Line 8) P.94
28	Sleep me	Knocked out by a punch	It Was Supposed (Line 23) P.98

INTRODUCTION

I'm a Poet and Ya Know It. Vol 1 first came into existence, in 2011, when I returned home to the Bronx, New York from Los Angeles, California. The return I felt, was a step backwards in my life, as I went from aspiring actor and a new life, to returning to one I sought desperately to escape from. Thus, I grew depressed and this depression would last three years, in which, I kept myself, secluded and avoided as much human contact as possible, except for work of course.

After staying a year and a half in Los Angeles, I returned home feeling a failure with nothing more than luggage of clothes and boxes of CD's of my Acoustic Rap album entitled, In Tune. Which I still have available for purchase *wink wink*. Ultimately, taking that huge risk of leaving it all behind, in New York, only to return home, to where I was born and raised, was heart wrenching for me. So in 2013, after writing fragments of uninspired rap lyrics for two years, I wrote a poem entitled: Pity. This poem was the first time in my life, that I was able to speak my truth, unapologetically! This one- time people pleaser with nothing but good jokes, laughs and good times finally admitted he sought your sorrow, all the while expressing how ridiculous that idea was!

I sat on Pity for a while and then I reached out to a good friend of mine and read it to him over the phone. His response was excitement and I said shit, we might mess around and have something here! I would rehearse it like crazy, memorize it and everywhere I went, I made an excuse to share it amongst friends and family and their responses excited me! I remember reading Pity off of my phone, to a packed Nuyorican Poets Cafe audience because I was too afraid to perform it. This was my first time reciting a poem in public to which I drew cheers from the audience. I frequented the Nuyorican Poets Cafe a lot as a teenager and admired so many courageous souls before me, so there applause meant a lot to me. It was for sure something that burned at my core to do but my fear outweighed my passion at the time. When I finally sat down, a young Caucasian male, who was sitting next to me asked me, hey was that really your first time reciting a poem? And I said yes! I had such low self-esteem at this time, I didn't know whether to take his question as a compliment or as an insult. But I guess it was good because I got an overwhelming crowd reaction!

My confidence grew from all of the positive responses and feedback that I had received. You see, I always wrote and still do but I was what you may call, an in the closet Poet, if you will. The kind that would never reveal his work to anyone but who would always be working on something! It didn't help that I surrounded myself with people who never really supported or encouraged my art! (Message)! Anyways, I began to write with a sense of conviction and purpose and I loved it! It was like I was reminding myself of who I was every time I wrote! I wrote until I had about 10 pieces that I could be proud of. Then in 2015, I shot a video for a poem that allowed me to expression my passion and rage. This poem was entitled, I've Created a Monster which you may also enjoy in this fine book and of which is my most viewed video to date! After I wrote this piece, I for sure knew I had something that was worth showcasing and sharing beyond just a phone call to a few friends.

So in, 2016 at The Point Theater, I took my 10 best poems mixed it with intervals of a mock R&B comedy skit group, called Hodeci (The knock off to the famed 90s R&B group Jodeci), in between, added a DJ and you had, Themilioxperience Presents: A Spoken Word Poetry Event Fo Dat Ass! The title is quite intriguing don't you agree? I just wanted to shake the cobwebs off poetry for many who felt this genre had fizzled out.

2017 was a big year in acting for me, as I was featured in shows such as: Blue Bloods, Orange is the New Black, Law and Order SVU, Blacklist and Elementary. I also starred in three off Broadway Productions such as: Sure Thing and Auld Lang Synge for the Lonely Planet written by Ted Talk Speaker Eunice Hudak. I also appeared on A Sketch of New York written by Joe DiNozzi and Darien Di Maria. All of these experiences helped shape my goal of Performance Poetry. Yet I was pulled back into Poetry in the classroom, as an Educator, Teaching Artist and thus writing proved to be a staple in my life and so here we are.

I'm a Poet and Ya Know It Vol. 1 is the culmination of Spoken Word Poems that I speak my truth, from its language to its content. It is the daring to be who you were always meant to be, deep down inside. It is allowing ourselves to be who we want to be unapologetically.

A good friend once told me, "When you are in your own lane there is no traffic" so this book is my vehicle.

! I hope you enjoy my body of work. Thank you for your intrigue, interest and support of this work, it means you help turn dreams into realities! Many blessings to you!

Fallen Angels

You've slipped through the cracks through open crevices, pot holes saved
By thorn like gloves that came to aid, to break your fall instead broke your heart

Like cracked egg shells leaking yolk, desperation choked like fire smoke
But you fell further

Met by falsehood, pretenders, propaganda
One hitter quitters and fender benders

Each prying away precious time like lions their prey, mutually invested days now gone astray

Devoured like a beast
But not before they dropped off a seed, huh like they was making a delivery

Falling where age betrays beauty

Supposed to fall hard, fall deep to bottomless, cynical, pits but it made no sense

The one door of love that opened up for you was enough to know that you have fallen in love with love

The feel was real and it was worth the hurt,

The starting all over again, the let's be friends, the let's see what he's really like if he really likes me

No mental fatigue from all the words that did forty yard dashes, jumping jack's and suicide drills

The fast talking that sold you passion in an un orderly fashion

That you paid for in cash

With no money back, guarantees

Spoken Whispers

You see, I ain't no scientist
But I know our skull is there to protect our brain

Then why doesn't it protect from the negative talk that slips past the
hard structure from contaminated lips

Teaching doubt and fear as direct as a spear

Grooming anxiety, so that when he grows, he'll have everything he
needs and will pray for but he'll never know because they never
spoke the tools for him to recognize them

Instead he believed in words like ugly, incapable, stupid,
incompetent

While others heard lullabies, he heard resentment about his cries

Upset that he wept, scared his tears into fear no self defense

Words that could've help to build, construct, instead took him apart
before he had a chance to be whole

But his love poked him like a bug, no matter what, nature calls

He made rhythms from the beatings that the spoken words
preached, giving his A Capella life meaning

He was no scientist but he furthered science

By building his brain a filter that blocked spoken whispers of death from ignorant lips

Burnt from human beings with the hatred of fire breathing dragons

But his filter was there to extinguish those flames that came

All because he remembered that a single spoken whisper can send you to your grave and in between life would have no meaning

You know, no ambition or drive, your ride in park with the boot on, your game on pause, no more Santa Clause for the kids, so all hope is gone

He went back into time and sung himself those lullabies the words that would've been second nature or natural instincts by this time

Because even words conveyed as a spoken whisper
That appear sweeter than sugar canes could be sharp as a guillotine

A soft spoken word like hate, could turn life into death

Slain, suicidal, depressed, anxious, nervousness, erasing confidence before it blossomed

Crushing like cinder blocks from rooftops (bad news) that strikes like lightning because when it rains it pours

Words are your weapons to build or destroy

His brain thought it, tongue was the culprit, brought it to the limelight thought it was his calling to be bold and stoic

Until self-control, lost control like a drunk driver at the wheel, his ignorance, incompetence could've killed

I guess he figures, "If your brain thinks you're stupid you must be" Who did you listen to, you choose

Did you buy my chip?
Is it installed in?
Or
Did you let evil win?

Cocktail Laughs

Why so serious?

Loosen up, stop being so uptight, life is great, it's right everything's grand my friend
I mean look at me, I'm fly, got a nice ride, live on the Upper East Side

My happy hour is every hour on the dot because everything's all right
I got laughs to throw away just for the shits and giggles

A smile, divided by work's classism, where the class system reigns supreme
Where struggle rubs shoulders with muscle
The poor showing remorse, hunger, fatigue

Wearing stress on their face like mascara

Holding on for dear life, while the others work but have lives
Smiles with mouths open wide, cocktail laughs on work time and we watch them like how do you that?

A laughter that can only be born out of sheer love of self and the circumstances that precedes it, the bed sheets one sleeps in

Shit before this I thought Ritz was only a cracker till I found the Ritz Carlton, Madison Avenue, Park Avenue, where every day feels like Christmas

Nobody asked me if I like the finer things, diamond rings no

Instead it's double the work and they get a coupon for our salaries half the pay
That shit ain't straight, not in the least bit, no way

The song's wrong it's not
Mo Money, Mo Problems
It's Mo Money, less hassle
Mo Money, Mo Ass Holes

Standing over the weak
Tongues moving, speaking commands like lasso lashings

The whipped, take the hit and thank God for every bit

I've Created a Monster

I've Created a monster (It's alive!)
Stitched his skin with a series of Y.E.S.' most definite

His ears were only made to hear, compliments
So each word acted as a pump inflating his head that later became
hard as a rock, stubborn

But he's our prince, could never do wrong
His scream played lead, singer to my ear drums and we made a
melody

Cradled him in perfect, wrapped in biased blankets of blind love
No one to edit, spell check or correct him
So he speaks a, foul language

Breath reeking of manure from all the shit he's talking
Fails everything but passes judgment, every time

Belly full of negligence cause if it ain't about him, he won't give a shit
Big lips and a mouth full of arrogance

Y'all could chill, kick it, long as your ass is the target, butt of the
jokes

Thinks the world owes him something, so his hands are the 24 hour
store because there always open
No class but he majors in finger pointing

He's superman with the power of unlimited favor requests
But he does you one and never lets you forget

Not an ounce of discreet on his person

His heart drenched in deceit and you can't tell him he ain't the greatest

I've Created a monster

Disrespect runs through his veins
His questions are commands
He's the best, short but looks down on everyone, a walking contradiction

Coughs bullshit
Allergic to sharing and caring
To negate him is hatin, so finger waving is forsaken
You've already gotten a whiff of him because ass hole is his fragrance and he wears it well

Favorite food? Sel-fish-ness
And Chucky, ain't got nothing on him!

He puts the con in conversation
He's bad for your health
His hot breath cremates, a pain in the ass
Disagreement, got him teething

Now the abomination of the Abominable Snowman, proclamation, manifestation, contemplation well it really doesn't matter what he's saying cause he's not much into practicing what he's preaching

But who could've imagined that a baby face could pack a leeches lips
Who sucks until a warm body becomes a cold carcass

His words are like a slit of the wrist, whispers death, hates anything that he can't get

Only prays to God cause he thinks he's God's gift then turns right around and preys on God's children

Now my home is where the hate is

Fear replaces peace

A warm home is now a frigid monopoly these are the cold hard facts

Now I'm dressed in handcuffs
Trying to get it back

Even got me a chauffeur, a police officer
Because I'll be God damned!

What about you?

Zombie Land

Either I'm being a little foolish
or they... look... human

Scratching their skins I think they got rashes
Smells of shit, I don't think they wash their asses

Hygiene not a priority
In fact it takes a back seat to pricked skins and facial expressions of
orgasmic relief
That pleasure pain

Attitudes just as stank as their stench as white puki lips on dark
colored skin, eyes glazed, smiles glossy, teeth?
Black and yellow, black and yellow, black and yellow, black and
yellow

Hair? Like there was no father to his style
Old Dirty Oily
Their mattresses?
The hard concrete, old urine infested blankets but they were happy

Their pillows?
Were their arms crossed extended
In a deep sleep as alcohol reeks and onlookers, look on crazy
But they sleep like a baby

"Don't wake me unless you got a pint of that.... get right!"

With their red bushy cheeks they walk slow, fixated on their fix
They wear their monkeys proudly on their backs like Ninja Turtle
back packs

Pain creeps, until they get what they think their bodies need, healed

As one long drag, drags them instantly, out of insanity, temporarily

They were outcasts (Outkast) but couldn't rap a lick
And they could sing if hoarse lungs were in

Too numb to protest shootings
They're too busy shooting up

Suicide, it's a suicide

Time, only showing up in bad hips and wrinkled skin

That dose was love
The way it damn near swept them off their feet
Eyes half asleep

They use cigarette smoke as incense
And that smoke cloud, clouds their addiction for a second

A calm before the anxiousness

It feels so good
To look this bad
Welcome to Zombie land

A Fine Ass Nerd

I need me a fine ass nerd

One who even when she upset, use big words like....... inept and erroneous!

Whose argument sounds so good that I be like.... You know what?

You prolly right
You prolly right!

Whose tights hug them legs so right
They produce mountain ranges for curves what a sight!

We gonna blow dynamite
A book worm, knee deep in intellect who
Knows how to carry a conversation

Intelligent, simple, basic

I mean she could cross you over, while doing a crossword puzzle
Talented

She's conscientious
Knows the difference between a debate and an argument

Dialogues over breakfast
Problem solves for lunch
Has a new goal, damn near every month
A home body not a hardly home

Whose fine hips compliment
Her savvy and wit
Angelic voice out of juicy lips

Her look is the scene
Body language is the movie
Defines the status quo
And makes glasses look sexy
Eye candy

Whose brain keeps me intrigued
And my baby won't degrade you, over her degrees

Not complex whose complexion just like my coffee
Light and sweet

She could flash me, show me her chest
Then turn around and play me in a game of chess

She adds to the cause not causes the grief
A great speller
I mean she never puts an I in TEAM

Our eyes fixated
Hooked like a good book

She could say a mouth full
But knows when to button up
Dress clothes

She's so sincere and stands like a deer

Knows but ain't a know it all

A Good Gawd!
Mixed with a Lord Have Mercy
Sexy

Butterscotch

I went to give a high five but there was no one to give me dap
Just left me hanging

Then like a miracle I discovered my other hand so I clap!
Round of applause cause I got my own back

You see you giving yourself a little too much credit
You can't fade me, I'm bald headed that mean I'm smooth

You don't faze me because static and friction takes two
And I already pressed pause and hit the mute button on you

So this went from an argument to you bitchin all by your Goddamn
self!

You see you thought had me fooled
Well I ain't your spark plug or a board to which to throw darts off

I have a way with words but I Am Performing Arts
So it only gets better when you see me in action

My body language speaks volumes guaranteed satisfaction

For those of you who, I may lose because you say it's too deep like six
feet in the grave
Just know

You gotta get down, to get up
Get low to get high
You got to know what's going down
To know what's up

A handsome brother with substance

God forbid I have a little confidence

They gonna say I'm arrogant, fuck it

Kanye West once said "I hope these light skin niggaz never ever, ever come back in style"

But I'm the walking status quo
They watch how I move
So they could know how to carry themselves

So if I ain't trending or trend setting then I'm setting the bar too low
A butterscotch brother such as myself
Got normal folks quoting poetry doe
Woah!

So remove the shades, take the blinders off
Because you listening with your bias on and not your ears

Motherfucker I'm ill that deserves cheers
If I didn't fit into your box of thought
Then you need more beers!
Because sober is the new intoxicated

Must be outside of your mind

Mind your words and your manners
Because my grammar is as nice grandma

This is just too dope to be cocaine
Simple an plain

Where's My Cape At?

I am the Kryptonite to hard, sharp, cut eyes and stares attached to evil lips

Whose every word is an incision like a knife, digging deep ready to kill
A person's spirit

Residing from mouths
Who gargle with jealousy and rinse with envy

So what is my weaponry you ask?
I am strapped with an automatic tongue, a rapid response

You can call it a knee jerk reaction, for anytime you happen to fix your lips to say some inferior shit....
To me

You know what?
Scratch that

If you even think some inferior shit
We battling mentally, telepathically and my mind will beat your mind up!

You see my words are the shield
Woven in courage and respect
So you better "put some respeck on my name"

Skin made of oil, so you're words won't stick
Plus I keeps a bottle of that bitch be gone spray in case they wanna play

So Where's my Cape At?
Cause I got big balls made of steel

My huffs and puffs burns eyebrows clear off

My tongue is a sword
Slaying foes with harsh tones
Plus I'm out here fighting the crime of negligence

Putting in the time so they won't have to do, time
So in due time, they'll flourish and at my old age
My world won't be filled with violent, degenerates

So Where's My Cape At?

Cause I got a justice league tongue and my saliva is the whole team
Cause I not only say it, I spray it

Giving back like a knapsack

There's just too many wicked spirits with hot breathes
That speak with conviction and nobody to return their serve
Until now

Giving the meek a voice
Allowing themselves the pleasure to offend a motherfucker
Who has no respect for them

Plus I keep a steel toe boot on, in case they want to practice getting
there shit kicked in

So Where's My Cape At? Cause you hate that admit it
If they don't change their new name will be:
Fresh off an ass Whoopin

Plus I can't stand it whenever somebody tells me
They can't change that's just how they is

Cool

Well I'm life's response to their shit

I'm the repercussion

I got middle fingers for belligerent, ignorant, niggaz
So speak with caution

Because I sever tongues that don't watch their mouths

I'm just policing my metropolis
When 911 needs....
911 called on them

It's a bird
It's a plane

Nah

Just a man
With justice for lips
Whose words arc his weapons

And enough action to back them

Wait

You see
I finally figured it out....

People would wait you know be patient
Really they would

But you see.. well... there's this thing

People love to hear the sound that their car horns make
Just as soon as the light turns green!

But they have a legitimate excuse
They have a disease and that disease is called:

IMPATIENCE

And they fear that that extra second
That they would have to wait
Would lead them to an early grave

I mean that wait
Could be the end of their fate
That red light has got to be green
I mean they're both dark color shades

That wait
it's just too much weight on their shoulders

That's why when their on line
right behind
You can feel their hot breath on your neck

One minute they're right behind you
The next? They're shoulder to shoulder

But it's a disease
So bear with them

Their world ain't like yours and mine, no
You see the hands on their clocks makes them dizzy, crazy
Still not sure of who they are?
Here are some of the symptoms:

Desperate to be next
Even breaking out in cold sweats
When they rush!
They.... get a rush!

Their always vexed, suck their teeth, tap their fingers and their legs
Throw hissy fits, ice grills, mean face
Their time is more important, in fact time doesn't move fast enough

Annoyed, distressed, talk under their breathe
They gotta get somewhere, have to pee, geez Louise, now luckily....
There is hope

Yup
I built us a cure, a human remote control

So now
When you press pause, they pause
Press stop and they stop
Rewind, fast forward but people are having too much fun

With slow mo (Slow Motion)
Slow motion for me, **slow motion for me, slow motion**

You see they walk like the wind,
In New York City
In fear
Because they swear that

Godzilla is coming out of the TV

That he's really chasing them in these streets
No make believe

They thought they could really get trampled
So now that rush comes to a halt, stop, Atten hut!

Nobody to bull doze pass or bum rush

You see things were going well
That is until people rapidly flipped through channels and between
popcorn and the couch they broke the remote and lost their minds
So people got out of control

With no patience in site killings, murders, protests, rise
Injustice, discrimination, thrive
They were taught that the world was theirs and everybody else was
just, in their way

Sped up on yellow lights and didn't believe in red
So they died just as fast as they came
All because they... didn't take a deep breath and....

Wait
.

Vanity

You look gorgeous, stunning, beautiful
Spoke by lips with a side of drool
Gave her all those compliments since he didn't know which one to
choose

To which she replied
I know

Ignored her mood

Instead, salivating at the thought
She knows I got a hold on you

And she carries on knowing she is the bomb

Vanity

A mirror hardly leaves her face as lurking eyes corroborate, her
already high praise of herself

Lips full, firm, cheek bones too, eyes wide, brown pupils

Long legs, slightly bald legged, curly hair that could always be
straightened for any occasion

Lust on every strut, flirtatious
Tearing the runway and the board walk right up, plump buttocks
Make up, to make up for whatever her brain and mouth
Make up

You couldn't believe it either maybe it's Maybelline or maybe not
Her beauty is all she's got, so she feeds her face with cream
But that make up backfired

As her skin grew old and tired from being misused

Suffocating pores

Relied heavily on her looks, until nobody looked

Never fed her brain, now her tongue got her looking insane

Since beauty is skin deep, she was buried alive...
A walking zombie

You see beauty never reached her internally, attitude ugly
The remnants of a spoiled brat spilling over
She had a chip on them cold shoulders

Only conversation she ever had was about herself
Would watch her own reflections while looking at yours
She held on to the days when eyes hawked, attention, consoled her
soul

That mean walk in them pumps with an extra swing on that thing
Eyes reeled them in
Until they were hooked like trout only to be gutted out

Fell in love with her beauty
Allowed that to take precedence

Neglected her attitude, ego amplified, inflated
Went from gorgeous, stunning, cute to ooh
What happened to you?

Couldn't help but stare at your magnificent hair
Skin smooth as a baby's rear, aroused from what's under that blouse
Thought beauty would over compensate

But life got ugly
A mere reflection of her interior
Where men brought her roses, to their own funerals

*So life had a funny way to repay, used her veins because her life
would go in vain*

*Now her days are that of a junkie
Old skin, raggedy, what a tragedy!
Ironic, I think not*

*For all the days. she drained away hearts
When she could've danced to their beat
Instead got them for everything*

*She was beauty, smooth, skin oily
I swear*

She smelled of strawberries, milk and honey

Meet Me in the Middle

Meet me in the middle

Where we hang up our egos like coat check and use pickup lines of encouragement to navigate us through the bullshit

Where the DJ, spins good vibes and we dance At Club Compromise

Where our worlds don't collide they combine and we happen to form like Voltron, Optimus Prime, Meet me in the middle

Where arguments become civil debates
And we can agree to disagree
Where we take a laxative to keep from being full of shit and mutual respect runs this bitch!
Meet me in the middle!

Where war becomes a battle of the minds, a game of chess
Where there's always room for dessert and we save you a slice of humble pie, ya welcome

Meet me at the cross section between patience and understanding

Where we air out our differences with pressure oozing out slow as a fart
SBD you know?
Silent But deadly

Where we form a unit, a team
Laying brick by brick the road to our dreams

Where I take what I know and mix it with yours and together we make momma's homemade Ice Tea
Mmmmmmmmmm

Meet me in the middle
Where goosebumps meets lust, touch, hot, fun and my every thrust is
a bulls eye hit

Where your moans are the music to my ears and our love is as loud
as a screaming orgasm!

Where we draw squiggly lines in the sand
Not hard, rigid, concrete one's, against one another

Where our hearts have ears, so our messages are loud and clear

Where we're even keeled
Balanced
Not too high nor too low
When life gets a little rocky yo

Where there's no need to call and ask where I'm at

Cause I'm at where I be and I be where I'm at

In the middle

Affectionate

I need affection baby
I need you to touch me with your eyes
Make me feel special lady

Make me feel like I'm your prize

Let's give our mouths a break and stare in each other's eyes
So we speak with our hands like we are mimes

Interrupt my statement, kiss me mid stride
Before I finish my sentence
Make me pause like a comma, momma fuck it

Take initiative, take the reign sometimes
Never deny me a kiss or ever hold sex as a weapon
Never dangle it in front of me like a carrot for a rabbit
I need affection baby

You at work all day? Fine
Text me with a flirt, a joke or damn it, something kind
Let me know without a doubt, that I am on your mind
Flirt with me

Cause you got to ignite that fire that later will blow your mind

You don't like to give massages?
Cool cause a back rubs just fine

I want to feel you baby
And I want you to feel me too
But I got a question?

Are we making love or lasagna?

Cause each has its own ingredients

Love?

Bedroom eyes, a dash of soft hot breath in our ears
Enough to raise hairs and make goosebumps appear

A punch of care, much patience and time
A bond, friendship, common ground
Something that makes us unite

A pinch of tongue
That savor lips... like that were made of
Ice cream

A sweet kiss, succulent, slow like
Taking our time never pressing rewind
Eating our bodies with kisses, a neck damn near Dracula bitten

I need affection baby
I need to know that I matter
That my presence is felt literally

Our mouths on mute but our communication?
Never falls on deaf ears
Fuck words, we reading each other's minds
Rubbing me the right way even at the wrong time

Allowing our bodies to talk it out
So affectionate that we can count the heartbeats off each other

My White T-Shirt

My white T shirt is like a big ass bib

Cause when I go to feed my mouth, my mouth says uh uh, we don't need all of it, let some drip!

You like to paint? Cool cause my White T turns into an empty canvas when I wear it

Except my colors are:
Fish grease and barbecue sauce, to go along with ketchup red and mustard yellow, marinara, tartar, ranch, chocolate

You name it, I've worn it on my white T shirt

But I can't be alone with my white T no cause it scares the shit out of me
I throw it on and I hear whispers of feed me, feed me

You see I throw on my White T in the morning and by evening you'd think I went rock climbing

Me and my white T made literal of the phrase "Dinner's on me"
But I have some nifty ideas for my White T
Shirtless in the summer? I use as a rag for washing cars

Or as a bag for vomiting purposes or as a mop
Don't have bounty? No problem

Clean your counter with my White T

You see it really doesn't matter
What you use it for the results are all the same

I throw it in the washer?

And I swear I could hear bleach laughing at me (ha, ha, ha)
(Motherfucker)

Oooh, ooh I know
Instead of washing my White T shirt after I'm done I'm going to
donate it to the poor so they could have three course meals all in one

You will be hungry no more and my white t shirt is the cure
With stains galore of fresh foods, fruits and pastries
An open sample menu

You no longer have to read it
You like it, grab it, eat it
Off my White T shirt

You see, I thought my White T was supposed to cover me, keep me
warm
Instead it turned into u plate that we could all stuff our face
I mean it's no wonder every time I have it on, pigeons hover, ants
crawl up and down it

They'll be days where I ain't even stain it yet and I already see ants,
pigeons and mice with napkins tied around their necks, tongues all
out their face
Just waiting for a taste

I mean any other color and I'm as clean as a nun at a convent
Not so much as a burp

But let it be white and I have oil stains, juices any flavor you want
I even got other people's food on my shirt

I'm convinced it's attracted to dust, stains, grease and dirt
A magnet to mice, allergic to detergents

Oooh I know food, grease and color
Just want to be friends with it

All week I kept myself clean
Until I threw on

My White T

Floodgates

Your pen strokes should've drowned you a long time ago

Your words was supposed to be the arc to get us through the storm
Instead you opted for the norm, mundane, same, fade
That nobody could recall

So I'm opening up the floodgates and you have two choices:

You could either, drown from its depths, you know
You know let it go over your head?
Or Swim.....

Either stay current or go against the current

You decide but there's a new flow in town

Better follow suit or get buried in one
Either way I'm opening up the flood gates
Because you're flows never made waves, ripples

So you can back pedal, do hard breast strokes
Even.. float but you will be mesmerized by the flow

Welcome it's bluntness, boogie board surf on it, bath in its
confidence Dive in, head first, bathing suit or not because although
the waters appear lukewarm

The waves allow you to cruise, set sail, remove the anchor that held
you down with a substitute, brand new, feeling inside, now, there
will be casualties

I mean it is a flood you know?

*Some will drown, they just couldn't keep up but your long strokes
won't go for not, no*

*Those, keep you afloat
Keep you..... in the know*

*So when the hard wind blows and you sense the flood coming
towards, warn the town's men, wife and kids, dogs, cats, civilizations*

*Get you an arc....oh wait...
That's already been taken*

*Well just warn somebody
That I'm opening up the flood gates and there ain't no damn that
can withstand.... yet...there's no need to be afraid*

*Cause the flood comes to sweep you off your feet like you were in
love with its ocean*

*It came to set the record straight with record breaks
Leave it's mark, with exclamation flows, one for the books*

Make HIS-TOR-Y

*It's ripples curb wrinkles
Keeps you sharp, young*

*You see, I've opened up the flood gates
An despite its turbulent arrival
You'll savor its freshness*

*Its innovative waters came to cool you, off
Although deep, it's meant to teach the open minded*

*Drown the redundant, who were hell bent on keeping things similar,
constant so make way
Fight against it and you will perish
Be outdated, obsolete, isolated*

So ride the waves of turmoil they call change

That you will initially deem as strange
But let the flood fall like rain in the drought

Rinse away your tightly screwed brains
Sooth away the pain
That will propel you to swim faster, harder

Away from monotony
Away from the dry desert plains, that fade us into obscurity

Today we separate the row boats from the jet skis
Ships from the submarines

So ready or not I'm here
Because the floodgates are open....

Settled

You woke up
Somewhere between soft tap kisses, mediocre sexual experiences and
lonely Monday mornings

Too many late night binges
Years creeping like nightmares
Scared of the little grey hairs forming that people keep reminding
you means wise but you don't feel so smart

No kid to call your own
No one to call on you

Stuck like Chuck or stuck with Chuck
You haven't decided yet

So you say well,
Attractive, friendly, steady sex and can screw a light bulb too?
Aww fuck it who am I kidding?

I do

You replaced gorgeous with cute
Sexy with tempting
Ambitious for well.... at least he got a job..shiit

As the years rise, that bar you've set so high
Begins to decline ditto for your confidence

Couldn't hear so well
I think you were screened by the wedding bells

Threw on that ring like a shackle
Dress feeling like a straitjacket and you're pretty sure these shoes
didn't feel like a ball and chain

When you first fit them on at the store?
(I'm just saying)

So you were late, trying to find the other half of your heart in time to
walk down that aisle see
You just wanted your words to be on the same sheet of music

I mean after hearing all that Jazz
You were ready to Rock N Roll to kick the Blues
Didn't listen to Rap until they called it Pop, mainstreaming
So you lacked much oomph, much funk
Let's rewind

Thought excitement was only to be coveted by children full of hope
and promise and yours was just supposed vanish into thin air
As if you were always an adult, if only you didn't inhale
This would've been, a whole lot easier

Your heart and brain argue and you stand there trying not to look
puzzled like
Is passionless companionship better than loneliness?
Or does two likes equal, love?
Or, or is like, a lot like, hitting the pause button on life, until love hits
home?

Trying like hell to muster up some authenticity in your wedding
photos
A photograph of circumstances

See this relationship is either false or hitting a falsetto, you know,
Opera like raging orgasms so much so you thought you had to toe
tag em because there was no saving him

But you are enslaved..
To thoughts instilled by your parents whose ideals coincide with the
opinions of those people who don't pay your bills yet who somehow
Control your will, run your feet, drive your wheels and rule your
feel.....

So you hit the road, riding shotgun with fear
All so you won't let down your folks, who put on the show to let you
go down that eight mile road...I mean aisle

You have settled and now there are kids in the middle
Smiles is like a game of pretend bored of the bullshit
Yet your mirror is the only one being honest

You thought you could escape it what your heart was craving
The yearning like hell to exhale, passion
The lust for lusting eyes leading to your clothes' demise

Raving with intensity
Hot breathe pressing your skin chased by soft, wet kisses
Enacting goosebumps, erect nipples and weak knees

Too much excitement to be contained
So Victoria's secret is a secret no more

But when the music stops and you're alone
Realizing that this is your life, that you did not control
The truth, is dug up, by your soul

You see reality came in and took the other room
Somewhere between a tough decision and the truth
Eyes are full proof

You just couldn't shake it
When the attraction started fading
What was once cute is now annoying
Eyes rolling

Thought about everyone else's good sense but left yours unkempt
Days became repetitive, monotonous
Because you knew he didn't bring you the flowers your heart was
craving
So hope, goes stripping like a pole dancer

See, you're face wore the aches that, he knew as you're face
He couldn't trace its roots to the beginning
Hadn't the history nor the chemistry
That when two souls dance
They catch each other up and fill in the blanks

Instead marriage, is now you're purgatory
As your sub conscious awakes in cold sweats and bitterness leaves
your lips
Afraid to face the music that once gave you life
Now gives you torment
Haunts your every moment

Thought you had hot....but life chilled ya
So you put it in your cup, filled it with Vodka and drank it up

Now a candle lit less dinner, alone, is the story of your life

All because

You have settled....

And left your heart alone

To fend

For itself

Chocolate

Let me ask you a question
Why every time I'm with you, I put on a little weight?
She said because I like my men with a little fat on em

Well ok, that explains that!
But damn it y'all
I think I love her
I'm telling you, it be me and her in the end if no one else understands

Yea I know her attitude switches
Could be a little different but my momma always said....
Life was like a box a chocolates....
You never know what you gonna get

She could be crazy, nuts like almonds or be simple and plain
She told me she wanted to role play right
So she came dressed in all White
(We're in love)

So I could have her anyway I want
But our relationship is sacred
I have her in the dark

Ours is deep
I get in touch with her roots
When we're alone? It's Cocoa

Chocolate is just more marketable
We're moving in

Cause I always have a taste, for her pretty milk skin
If we ever broke up I'd be in pieces like peanut butter was in em

You see she's a model

And her body belongs in them glass bottles
they carry her in

She fills them out perfect
Turns me on
She's my aphrodisiac

And it's so hard, to stay away, and be celibate
It's like she won't let me quit
No matter the day I'm having
She always saves me a kiss

I go away on business?
She's on my pillow as soon as I get in

Gotta contain myself before she raises my sugar
But damn it y'all, that's my shooga

You see, she knows she's sweet
Tastes good
Real yummy

Looks good all by herself
But brings her fine ass friends
Soy, Sugar and Caramel

I need her and won't ever let her go
She just can't know she has so much control

When I make her heart melt
I make me a s'mores
She adores so she goes on all fours

Chocolate is so beautiful she's damn near perfect
Goes with everything, wafers, coffee, pretzels

I mean she has her own float, ice cream, commercials

We riding, yea I give her a whirl
Finger licking good when I'm with my girl

And we'll never go broke cause she always sells
She's fine and rich
As hell

Chocolate

Desperation

Nothing sweats like desperation

Sweaty sap sticking
Pepe le pewing up the spot thought it was love
It was not

In fact it was closer to harassment
Cause you just couldn't get away

And it always happens that the pursuer looks
crazy, baby
Unshaved, unkempt, ill mannered,
Temper tantrums thrown for called strikes

In The Show*, it's three strikes and you're out
But life is like the NCAA Tournament
One and done

So ya better get it right the first time
Sho ya right!
Before blue and red lights haunt ya ass like the Poltergeist

Nothing sweats like desperation as perspiration drips
Pepe le pewing up the spot blowing her cell phone up

Now you're blocked and she's got proof
Indicting yourself with hate voicemails

Should've jailed those thoughts and kept them to yourself
Now you're in jail cleaning pots, playing with ya self

But she was a bitch!
Oh yea?

Well ya gonna need a new pitch and a lawyer
Because the bases are still loaded, to coach you out of this
predicament, player

Nothing sweats like desperation as perspiration drips
But you're too anxious
She thought you had the juice but really you're just thirst

It's a damn shame
You not on your game, lame
It's a psychological warfare
But you're not interested in standing your ground

Trading verbal jabs of confidence
Defending your respect no

Instead your plan is to be pussy over pussy
Only she ain't no lesbian and don't need no more estrogen

Nothing sweats like desperation as perspiration drips
Trying to fit a hoe with a crown
And she's like wow

Watch out now

Now your relegated to a sucker

Motherfucker

Top of the Totem

So you made it, all the way
Made it to the top of the food chain
Dug yourself out of the rut
Out of the shitter, congratulations!

You worked hard, tireless, shoe shining egos
Even found a home for your big, fat lips
On flat, droopy, hairy asses

You hated your name because
"English please, this is America!"
Kept mis pronouncing your name

So you took the accent off your accented name
So they could pronounce it proper and when you get a chance you
will change your name to fit their pronunciations

Meanwhile you learned to wear a cheesy smile on your face
As foul as pork
Especially when ain't shit funny

Spritzing your skin with cockiness and even bleached your speech

As you came back to your old stomping grounds
Because in that business world you were an afterthought
And in this one, you can show off your princely robes to standing o's

You feel you are somebody people should admire
Because your ego caught the blue balls in between THEIR walls
But here you can get it stroked, spit at and swallowed, for half off

Congratulations!

*But somewhere in between our salute and praise our words got
mistook for bowing deep on our knees
As if inferior, slaves*

*Our friendliness and kindheartedness became your red carpet
To step all over with brand new, brand name shoes
You got from the clearance rack*

*Now you are an alien displaced
Without acceptance from the other world you tried feverishly to
integrate into and the place you left, you now feel is beneath you*

That your mother

Still calls

Home

Almost Famous

Fed up, so he swam in a pool of fuck this shit and drank a half a cup
of discontent
About his situation

So to soak away the pain?
He made a concoction:
Took:
An idea, gave it a little thought, put some action behind it, discipline
And Bang!!!
He became a......
Pro (Pro?, Pro)
No Crastination

All because he burned his warm bed sheets of laziness
And the matching pillow set of justification
Who wanted him to sleep right through loud alarm clock sounds of
alert

Who wanted him far, far away
Where dreams turn into nightmares of regret
Haunting his consciousness with voices
Because his calling was never answered

So they left a message
And he made every excuse in the book about why he didn't do
What he really wanted to do

Now he's a dad who force feeds his kids
HIS passion
But they never really acquired a taste for force feedings

Instead he pushed his kids so hard
That he pushed them away

All because he hit the snooze button of excuses about his life like:
Not today, boring, it's too late, wait, I'm on my way!

So he pump faked, hesitated, for so long
That his bones became brittle and his youth disappeared like magic
Vanished

He could've helped the world
But he just, couldn't get off his ass
You see his seat had crazy glue on it
Don't you just hate when that happens?

So he remained seated heated
With only bitterness and complaints, to leave his face at an old age
You were almost famous

But YOU CHOSE to believe

I Can't
So...
I QUIT
Became your stop sign

As you were hugged by failure and kissed by embarrassment

So you left before the check came
Because you felt you
Didn't need to pay your dues

Didn't want to take the time to prepare your home cooked meal
So you chose fast food and made fast fools

Of all those who took the long road on that rainbow that now swim
In their pots of gold
But you're special

So special that problems were supposed to make a left, circumvent,
stroll away leave you unscathed
No bumps, bruises, marks or scrapes

You almost made it
But you thought you'd only ever hear crickets
Where cheers await

Instead you allowed the naysayers
To land their haymakers

And a chorus of boos to be your theme song
In fact you joined them
In bashing you

And you figure "If I have a team at least I'm not alone"
So they saved you a seat because misery loves company

You were Almost Famous

But you decided to be afraid of what everyone else would say
Took THEIR opinions
About YOUR life and
You didn't want to disappoint them

Now all you have left is your word
That's been lathered in bull shit
Since the beginning

About what you

Could've been

Vanity II

She welcomes the hard erect stabs that prick
Penetrating her hot, throbbing body
Screaming ecstasy with every inch
She likes it rough

So disregard the marks
Why the lust for touch, deep thrusts?
Keep up because her ejaculation is times ten

She feels it deep
As dopamine creeps and sweeps her damn near off her feet
Every time like clock work

It's an everyday search
Every girl can be a slut to her man
And she's his

Until that mirror reflected her horror story
Came from glory was a Queen
The wife of a King
Had it all trips, jewelry, resorts

Nice eats, suites
Dresses, pearl necklace
A life you can only dream

Did it all with her beauty
Now her fanny?
Lost it

Aired on the side of caution

Her life was the price
That's what her new love costed

A once smooth skin turned rugged
Old disgusted
Unrecognizable
Yet held tight to justification

You know the one that tells you if you turn to this side
At this angle you're not fat, you're fine!

The same one that makes killing seem cool not mean
Especially when the victim didn't have it coming
Hunting for sanity in syringes
Damn near finished it

She got a fixed hit
Devastating

But her heart won the race, so fast
Then halted

Never to resurface

Again

Candle

In this crowded room
It's only us right now

Dancing to our own beat
Sweet caresses on those cheeks
You see

As the sparks fly, we allow the remnants to ignite our flame, hold it

As sweaty palms and butterflies lay claim
Take their place and stuttering follows so make way

I, I, I, I,
I think
I Love you

One candle, two hearts, a mutual responsibility to..
Keep on that spark so...
Flame on

Flowers, sweet kisses, establishing friendships, listening, speaking,
trust, interacting, the unexpected card, the showing love just
because

Celebrating each other in between birthdays and holidays
Home cooked meals
Back rub, foot rub, massage
You know the deal

She won your heart

It's only right you, show her what she's won

And when the candle wax drips

You do with it what you want

The call so she knows you were thinking of her,
You see, we were making love way before the glove*
As our bodies grooved to tunes
Our eyes perused and studied each other's moves imagining

Couldn't help but to help yourself
Lips far but close enough to close the gap
Because our eyes speak facts
Huh!
Already handled that

Back rub, massage, leaving the toilet seat down
That candle that now over looks your prepared dinner for her

There.... she.... glows
And takes claim of the flame
As the sparks fly, she pulls up your tie to your new function
A long kiss goodnight

Don't know what gets the better stroke your ego or what's in
between your thighs
Rise and stand tall

Pitching tents but you're not sleeping in any parks
The onslaught of support
The one your heart always sought

Gifts showered
Those lips, lavished, ravishing
Lingerie, foreplay

Desires, fantasies all meet in one day
Sexting to preheat home cooked quickies
Keep it exciting, sexy, craving

Built upon the grain

She sacrifices for the afternoon game

Watching

As your cheers are met with half a care
But she loves you so, there!

Couldn't be happier as can be
Two tickets to the opera
As she loves Broadway wants candy, you shower her with candy

Long walks on sand beach with a rented Yacht to propose
Her heart beats out of control
Her tears are the example
Happiness flows

Now you're both on your knees as she's weak can't even speak
But mustered up a yes filled weep

Eyes misty giving even the manliest man tears for a change
Renewed vows lovers and friends
Both wanting each other all over again

Re igniting that flame
Never allowing a night to go by without being able to rectify
Look each other in the eyes

Leaving no room for any other to light their candle
Because you

Are my fire!

Got To

How bad do you want it?
How bad do you want your dreams to be your reality?

Well
You got to have

The heart of a lion, be resilient, determined, undeterred
You got to be self-motivated

You got have a steel chin, Hercules' arms and a Samurai's shin

Got to have toughness, grit

Got to have
Will , skill and
A disciplined work ethic

Go to be willing to go the extra mile
Do it when nobody is around

When there ain't nobody to cheer you on and make you feel strong

Got to know
No
Got to have confidence
Even when life shakes it

Got to feel it, taste it, describe it
At a drop of a dime
Got to see it
Even when your eyes are too blind

No fear
Persistence, perseverance

Got to be brave
Got to talk it like you walk it
Got to want it like your life, depends on it

Stalk it, scream it, dream it, eat it

It's got to be on your mind, all of the time
You got to be in love, lust, crush with it
Married, engaged have kids with it

Got to want to do it, when you don't want to be bothered
Even when you are tired

You got to live it, love it, be it, believe it

It's got to be attached to your hip
It's got to be your everything

First love, second love, girlfriend, fling
Jump off, Main

If you cheat, it's got to be with it

It's got to mean more than a wedding ring
Your whole life, wife and you got to be loyal to it

Got to make time, when there ain't time
You got to have patience
Trust in the process

Understanding
Got to be enthusiastic

Rest less
Got to be ready to make sacrifices

Even willing to die... for it

Then and only then will you get to taste a piece

Of heaven

Clean

I'm taking in this town in my fresh, new, hand me downs

Prior I was in the shower

Trying like hell to scrub poverty off
With a steel dish washing scrub

And it's hard as a mug
But I'm gonna try

Using a bar of soap as my microphone I sing
"Ain't nobody dope as me, I'm just so fresh so clean, so fresh and so
clean, clean"

Fresh like meadow scent
Like I came right out the plastic
Dusting Salvation Army's finest
Because anything worth keeping
Is worth keeping clean

Using daddy's slick talk
I'm clean as a caddi-
Lacking nothing

Deuce, deuce and a quarter
On that Chevy Impala

Hands greasing the brim of my fedora
It's all over

So I shows up
For the show down

Fight, shining moon bright

Is why I got my shades on at night

Clean talk because my kind walks with two strikes
Shit, shave, shower and shampoo, I clean up well

I train my ass off
So I could scrub with force, hard like I'm starting a fire
To get poor off

So we could get poured up and celebrate by getting our pour on*
I guess that's why we get poured up*
To numb the problems that pour on...

I keep my nails clean
Cause she won't let you touch her, if you're hands dirty
Dirty!

So I'm well kempt
Best foot forward in my latest steps*
Like I'm meeting the president

This that bop
That limp for no reason

Some ice grills*
A few mean mugs*
That I Nyquil sleep on
Cause Hip Hop taught me
1, 2 and Ya Don't Stop and
Ya Don't Quit

Just keep pushing
Especially when things look disgusting

So I trot
Get my swerve on*
I take it in

Remembering

Why I bare all on stage like a stripper
To leave not one word unsaid
That before my death, I had lived
Soared for one night
Long enough to kiss the sky
That I leave nothing behind in my mind
Not even my opinions because if we can't take anything when we go

Then I, put it all on display and accept all of the criticism that should come my way

Even if it ain't always

Clean

Pity

If you take pity on him maybe they'll ease up

Not make it so rough, so tough
Just like he thinks he needs it

To see if he really means this stuff about wanting more and fighting
for
Doing whatever it takes, even if it aches, bakes, our breaks him in
half

Insane mad
To the point where he contemplates suicide missions like
Bombing at the Apollo

You must be out of your cotton picking
Outside of your jurisdiction
For thinking of optimism about you hitting*
Boy please

You better off playing lotto
Cause time is borrowed
So you better strike fast or die slow

But when you rise, cheers will fill your ears
You dip, slip, even just a little bit and the world will torture
Whatever's left, after they've torched your best

Discredit your name
Defame your name
You can cry the rain

But the shit better makes us move our hips
Think, flip, laugh or it's your ass
Mr. Postman

Because your delivery was a soliloquy but you didn't believe

No, instead you wanted us to feel bad for your dreams that haven't
seen the light
Wanted us to stop in our own tracks, forget our own past, that still
hurts like a fresh slap (Slap!)

All so you wouldn't endure a tear on your eyelash?

Well excuse me as I laugh
As I bypass
Get on this train, get on my way
Cause I've cried rain, swallowed pain and had no money for the
anesthesia

I learned the rules of life real quick like
You better get over it real quick

Two options
Either feel bad about your condition
or use it as motivation

And oh yea
You're allowed to cry man

Soak your tears in satin or cheers
Bounty or beers
But we all meet the inevitable*... once

So stunt, front or act like you're man enough or it's man enough

I'm sick and tired of hearing, just how sick and tired you really are

So life calls your bluff, to see if what you say is really what you want
Tests you until you question everything

Thought you were strong enough

But weight rooms, hold no weight fool

You needed to lift your brain to higher plains
Structure your frame to endure the pain
But keep your brain on the aim and never sway

Not going against the grain

But going against the part of the brain that wanted more

Pity

The Rent Money

I'm gambling with the rent money baby....
Fuck it

Yup, you see, this next hand is gonna be my best hand
I'm all in
Everything on black
I don't care if I have a royal flush
Or
A flush of the toilet

Because living like this, just ain't living
In between walls of lost and forgotten
Between would've, could've, should've and never made it happen
No

I'm splitting
Before these walls close in and crush my nasal passage
Fixed for smelling, sandy white beach front homes with miss jones

Crushing, fast heart beats of excitement, from taking my little sister,
nieces and nephew on shopping, sprees

Crushing my mother's keys to her new home, retirement funds
Crushing Christmas to those children who never felt it
Whipping up a taste of hope, so they could make it themselves one
day

The rent money baby
Because we need us a bigger place
Real Estate

A mortgage, so we could say, "this is our place"
Owned like a slave master

So this number is either gonna put us over or put us under

But all of my eggs are in one basket
Plans A-Z, all on a roll of the dice

You get, one of these to live and since we don't know when nor how
It's gotta be fun some way, some how

The rent money you see?
Baby, it's gonna happen for me
Because if it don't

Then the landlord better do knuckle pushups because he will be
knocking on my door till they're numb

But poof, like magic I go deaf, I go dumb
You send me a bill I send it right back

"Oh excuse me, I didn't see
Silly ol me"

The rent money baby, I know this sounds like the blues
But it's more like the green because you best be, cutting the check,
CTC or else

You see my comfort zone is starting to feel like rust and cold
Dry facial expressions, monotone
Oozing of deprivation and desperation

Like being alive but not living
Just surviving

Trading it all for, a reality check
You know the one

That zaps a dream's realization
But supports a survivor's slow deterioration

So it's the rent money baby

It could all go, gone, just like that
But I don't give a rats ass, just like that

Cause I've seen the bottom and bounced up, (snap) just like that!

You see playing it safe, scares me
Lacks the thrill of frills

That home run trot
That end zone, celebration
Ha!

You know the drill
Sound the Jack pot
Que the house to yell, winner!

And cash me the fuck out
So I can put a down payment on my new life

Set it straight, set it right
Be the best rich somama* bitch you ever did see

No entitlement, just setting the precedent integrity, respect,
humility, love, care and sucker free*

The rent money because living in rent controlled, cockroach, mice
flow in and out without paying rent

Just leaving behind their excrements
Just ain't for me

So give me the rent money
And hit me 21, I'm done
Somebody tell my J.O.B. to memorize my A.S.S.

Cause it's seen my back side, for the last time

Unless they cut on the TV and watch me exit......

The stage

Hell

It's raining bullets!
But I don't remember that being on today's forecast?

They offered to dry us like clothes on trees but the rope squeezed
tightly
They asked rather matter of fact if we would be the tree's Christmas
ornaments

"Sure I's be your ornaments Massa"

Hungry and I ate sleep
Stomach grumblings are my beats
Now your tattoo reads
R.I.P.

Jails filled with teenagers who smoke trees
Where they use to hang them from

7 day work weeks
Same 12 hour shifts
No time to be sick

A shiny badge blinds
As murderers steal lives

Need squeezes the meek
Now desperation seeps

They say looters make losers
But how else do we make,
What they do
News?

Hell

Slick

Slick so
You ain't gotta put her on
On the goings on of the room cause.....
She already scoured it before you knew what hit you, quick fast

Behind her partner's back
Her eyes robbed a glance,
From inquiring eyes, a wifed up* gentleman

Who was bored as shit,
Quiet as kept
Already shares something in common with her....
Eagerness

Who's fresh off an argument with his mate
An her words are starting to sound like blah, blah, blah, blah, blah,
blah, blah to him

There infidel eyes met
Locked, long enough to communicate,
Interested
A simultaneous "bathroom break" wink, wink, explains it

His number miraculously appears on her phone like

Hey, how'd that get there?

Slick but
I ain't stupid

I know how it is
He slipped, fell and landed on her clit
Sounds like a perfectly good explanation

You see her curiosity damn near killed her cat
All because she packs
Deep gazes
Provocative made of desire and flirtation
For every man, that she finds attractive

A kid in a candy store
Attention whoring on the strip
Works those thighs and those hips
But don't worry, she cleans up quick

Keeps a bottle of perfume around to block the stench
Left by foreign hips, who scratch her itch*

Gorgeous
With a face full of promiscuous

Now ain't that a bitch?
Or a ho?
All because she told multiple sex partners that this is yours daddy
So their excitement over joyed and they put in over time
She thinks she's slick but the truth

Always surfaces

They worked her middle
And it makes perfect sense cause
She's self-centered

Trades in sex for compassion

Just wants to be liked, admired, appreciated but her vagina keeps on taking all the lashes
Let's her eyes talk provocative

You see miss thing don't miss a thing

Couldn't contain her excitement, salivating at the vaginal secretions,
leaking from all the attention that once left her starving

So her eyes fished* constant

She's fast, hot ass
Middle finger to her mate
Out of sight, out of mind
Just wants to live her life!

Mentality
"Quit judging me, you never walked a mile in mine"

Her mama's cold heart left her naked
So she reveals flesh to gain attention

Trades in sex for compassion

Just wants to be liked, admired, appreciated
But her vagina keeps on taking all the lashes
Because tall, dark and handsome leaves her gasping
Everybody's got a story

Just make sure you're life
Don't prevent mine..... from living

A Letter to Laziness

Dear Laziness

How can I put this?

You...... are the Devil!

Now don't get me wrong, we had a good run!

It was so much fun doing absolutely nothing while the house went to disgusting

And when the super just so happened to "forget" to turn on the heat
You held me down with warm blankets and quilts

On second thought that does sound kind of sweet
But not when the trash reeks and you got to spray Febreze just to sleep
Instead of waking your punk ass up and taking out the damn trash
No, we have a problem!

You groomed me to sleep all day
Eat what I like not what I need

Giving me nothing but uncombed hair, bad breath, smelly feet and yellow teeth

You even gave me permission to get angry if I find myself outside of my comfort zone
Knowing damn well that outside of my comfort zone is growth

You made half asses out of great potentials

Made the bare minimum look like somebody's prime

We became the: Athletic Fat Asses

Is that a team? It should be
I think I'll trademark it

You made days seem meaningless
Because fatigue was your King
And you rather be beheaded than bend the knee (Game of Thrones)
Witcho lazy ass

What you gonna do when you propose
Huh? Huh?

I know misery loves company
But I don't see no ring on this finger

Instead you was a phase, a fling
So go ahead and do your thing without me

No, no you see your bullshit won't soar because it don't live here
anymore
From now on your bare minimum is gonna leave you bare
Ass naked or assed out you choose, you decide

Say remember that one time when you swore up and down
That you got your main sources of protein from potato chips?

You know you did stop lying
You did say that
You see

This is why we don't get along anymore
Because I'm sick and tired of all of your lies
Plus I got more fish to fry and all we ever do is eat chicken on repeat
It's like life is on repeat

You are the Anti Vitamin C

The roadmap to obesity
Footsteps to cancer
The how to be a dead beat
Mommy and Daddy

I'm turning another leaf
See where my best takes me

Because your lazy ass had me in shackles

Getting fat and real comfortable with the idea of having absolutely
nothing

And you see well responsibility bit me in the ass like you wouldn't
believe!

You wanna know what's better than you?
Being active, productive, hell a sense of accomplishment
It feels so good to see what I'm made of straight up

You tried to substitute my youth for wrinkles and joint pains
No
Thank you

Instead I work
You snooze I cruise
While your asleep I chase the best of me
Prime Time, Action, National TV

So give me the light
And watch me turn fifteen seconds of fame

Into an eternity

Ok with Uncomfortable

We exhale danger

It's hysterical laughter's in the face of bastards
And inhale hope

You rock our boat?
We Jet Ski through the waves
Spike our punch and we remain Kool-Aid

We're ok with uncomfortable
We just won't be rattled
We counterpunch the jabs that you throw at our confidence

Your hurricane of misery won't rain on our parade
Blind just means brail and we won't break cause we ain't frail

Deep breaths to de stress cause
It only gets better from here

What you call Parkinson's Disease we call rhythm
Thanks Tom Hanks

We're ok with uncomfortable
We take lightning quick breaths in between your antagonizing
And remain as cool as a fan in the shade

Anger us? And it's
"Live from the world's largest hands, it's the middle finger!"

But.... we express it to you, in the most respectful way possible
A skill
Damn near an art form

Wanna know how?
I'll sell you the answers
Even coach you out of your circumstances

We're ok with uncomfortable

Cause what other choice do we have?

Life can go berserk
But we won't go with it
Magnificent

So much so people ask
How do you do it?

And we say well
When you've faced near death experiences?

Yea, I think you start to pay attention

We're calm but the power of God is responsible

So all praises due to the most high

Thank you

The Power of Language

Speak

And throw words at them

Because the tongue carries much weight
It can unlock the scared that would've lived their lives tucked in
their shells
Or
Turn those same shells into shields and their tongues into swords
The Brave

Dug from out of a cave from out of the grave
Into a life where the sun brightens their face, into a smile

Alliterations curbing illiterates

You see their words were their seeds
The saliva from their mouths was their rain
That grew confidence, plowing their brains
Harvesting their minds until they feel fine, adequate

And you ain't said nothing but a word

You are what you imagine and words are your magic
Black or white
That could either conjure up or demolish
The Power of Language

Will make you comprehend even if you don't understand

The words that are coming out of my mouth!

Either they massage your eardrums or
Drum you at your core until your rattled

Communicating axes at your heart

Splitting it in half or putting it intact
Words

That even if you gave your back to the deaf
They would fully understand it because your tone
Speaks monsoons

Cracking pavements
Rumbling the earth

Your breath, would bring strong winds with it

Comprehension

Through your tones vibrations

The Power of Language

Cloud of the Ghetto

There seems to be no belief in the Ghetto

It's as if misery smoke clouds their better judgement
Even right now somebody's hating on this poem

Pessimism

Dressed in sayings like
"Yea, yea, you can dream but in reality are you really gonna make
it?"

You lose them when you switch it and say something like

"In reality I dream and in actuality I study and work my ass off until
I am accomplishing that dream!"

They take minor falls and bruises as quits and losers
Only choosing to see setbacks as red flags like it's over
Ya!

Dreams are reached everyday but they choose to replay the
Martin Luther King Jr assassination

People have asked me
Does this make them mean or angry?
I said maybe

But mostly I think it's ignorance covered in fear

You have challenged their marginalized faith in themselves
Many whose dreams they've quit because their environment only
supported their failures and nothing else

So they could all joke and laugh at you at the next bar be cue

The ghetto whose only foresight is dirty hallways and the smells of pissy elevators

Dreams are foreign too often told to
"Wake up because this is all that you will ever see!"

Spirits breaking in twos and threes
And
"You won't amount to anything just like your Daddy!"

Disease infested words burning holes
In their children's hearts and craniums
Pissing away hope

When their dreams are the only thing they have left to motivate them
I guess only the strongest survive

But we were taught to listen to our parents
Yet

Who would've imagined that the Ghetto's breastmilk

That was supposed to make us big and strong

Was poison

All along

Cloud of the Ghetto

Ignorance is Running This Bitch

Lest we forget

That ignorance is running this bitch and pride disguises it
Talking bout

"I know the shit that you speak of
In fact I knew this all along"

Because being wrong is being stupid, idiotic
Disregarding that each head is its own world and how they see the
shit
Zero for patience

And yet your ego tells you

"Yea, you knew it!
Your smart they're stupid
You're the greatest
They are just anuses
You don't need them
They need you"

Then life slaps you across your fat ass with a fat dick
And says why are you sad?

And your ego says work, attain riches!
And the self asks
Why are you sad? And the ego says

Work, work, work, work, work, work!

And gluttony got you a fat gut and mad bucks in your pocket
Then you realize you made it to the top and there's no one to cheer
you on

Thought you had friends but you never built any bonds
Instead you expected everyone to be exactly like you and all else was bull
Zero tries at comprehending

Anything outside of you
Selfish

And they all got F's on your test yet they had no clue you was a proctor
PROCTOR!!!

And arrogance told you
You look good but got no looks, likes from the world
So narcissism grew

Because ego told you
You are gorgeous and their just hating
But the self-asked why are you sad?

And ego disregarded saying work
And now your rich with no one to share it with

Because life told you
You get what you give

But all you ever did was take….
Advantage

And life saw a tire
Where you saw six pack abs

Saw a cringe
Where you saw a bright beautiful smile with white teeth and dimples

Saw hate
Where you saw constructive criticism

Saw rushing
Where you saw patience

Saw the movie saw, where you saw

A fairytale ending

Let The Bullshit Subside

You cloth your insecurity with pride and stack them sky high
Until your pride is higher than mine

To my chagrin you win and we both lose

When all it would've took was an apology while you work on your
inside

But you neglected it because you are so perfect
Ignorant and lazy

Not knowing better and never wanting to know any better either
And we must all gotta respect it

All because your greatest fear is to become vulnerable
Yet you forget that we were all born naked

It's like looking in the mirror and not seeing a reflection
If you can't face who you are
Who are you really facing?

You brave...really?

It's ok to take the mask off
Even Jason did it

Tears don't mean weak
You can still be adjacent to greatness

It's just you see
We got this soul that needs clothes
But like a deadbeat you neglect your responsibilities
And instead
Dress up your insecurities

I'm Platinum in the Shower

They said I can't sing...
Shit

Did my silk rhythmic words fall on deaf ears?
I blow like a saxophone
My windpipe harbors a tornado

I'm Platinum in the shower
What you think
I couldn't hear you trying to record me through the door?

They say where's the proof you ain't sold one record?
I said so what!
When my words erupt they supply the cool to the water
The vapor to the hot

It ain't that I can't sing
It's that I ain't been discovered yet!

It ain't my fault that these talent scouts couldn't find my house

I told them I'm at the corner of:
If Drake could sing, I could sing too Avenue
And
I'm Just Saying Road

But they claim they don't know what to do with me
I'm tall light and handsome
Two out of three ain't bad, shit
So figure it out!

I ain't marketable, I'm remarkable
That means you could do it again

I ain't here to do your job

You go make it happen!

But I'm Platinum in the Shower

So you know my bathroom is fit for a King
Shit that's at least the cover of Forbes Magazine
Or
Lifestyles of the Rich and Famous!

You see I came to reign
Every day I celebrate and there is no waste
Cause even my drain gets champagne

I'm a veteran so it's not like we gotta start from scratch
Because after my voice cracks
They'll be plenty of snatch, paychecks and all that
So find me a track asap so we can speed up the process

In the meantime
I'm gonna let this shower head be my microphone and this bar of
soap be my cordless
This shower cap be where the poet draws all of it

I blow like Coltrane after the rain

They said well if you could sing
Then how come I ain't never seen you on stage?

Well
 Because
  Like I said

I'm Platinum in the Shower

Dodo brain!

The Day I Found Out That Beautiful Women Farted

As the water glistens all over her bawdy*

Her with all those curves and me with no breaks
(That line sounds better in Spanish)

Her smile like it's only meant for me and her teeth damn near
blinded me
That shine, that sparkle, that beauty
Oooh wee
Put it in the air!

We stopped and stared and oh ya it was about to go down
Town

Until she needed to go to the bathroom
(Fart!)

Oh hell nah
And I was in the next room?
(Fart!)
Oh what the....!
(Fart!)
Ewww
(Fart!)
What the hell!?

I thought only men farted?
(Fart!)

This is unacceptable!
Weren't we the only ones that was supposed to be disgusting?

(Fart!)

Oh God, what was that?
Scared me so bad
My pants went (crap!)

You see I didn't want to start a competition

Cause I felt I didn't have enough ammunition
Besides this was supposed to be a sexual exhibition

I ducked and ran and that was that
Scared out my ass (and that's a fact)

And she must've been scared out of hers too
Because after all that gas
I didn't expect her to

Have a back

I grabbed my clothes like
What to do!?
Through them on, damn near forgot my shoe!

Scared for my life
I was scared I ain't gonna lie!

But she was so fine
Hurt my pride and heart

All this makeup and six pack abs
Great waist, beautiful face
And it turns out she's human... just... like... me

But these damn commercials got me thinking she was a fantasy!

It frightened but I guess I'll be alright

But if I ever see her again

I'll just be sure to bring the wipes, Yikes!!

Alley - Oops

In the land of ball hogs and low IQs
I'm throwing alley - oops

Off the backboard, massive, slam dunks
Classic
But you gotta catch my drift
Not drift off

So you can say you witnessed
This once in a lifetime experience
Halley's Comet

We taking flight skyrocket and we connecting in the air like
Shaq and Penny
Harden and Capella
Nash and Amare
Kempt and Payton
Wade and James

I'm throwing Alley - Oops
Cause when you score we soar
Making it look pretty because winning is sexy
I'm throwing alley - oops

Cause I love ball
So I let it go and if it's meant to be
I get it right back

I'm throwing alley - oops
Because you needed a jolt of energy
You gotta get up, get up, to get down

This that new pick me up
We replacing coffee

I'm throwing alley - oops
Cause I need a couple oooh's and ahhs

Whenever I'm winning

So after this gimme
We're doing the Mark Jackson shimme
Let me feel it!

I'm throwing alley - oops
Because there ain't no mistaking our greatness
And we're made for TV, so you can witness what I'm saying

I'm throwing alley - oops
For every player who gets froze out the offense , ice cold
But is expected to make the big shot at the end
I got you

I'm throwing alley - oops
Cause I want us all riled up, ready
Momentum building

Showtime like Magic and the Lakers
I'm throwing Alley - Oops for whoever catch my drift, ya dig?

Cause you gotta spike those Faulker!
It's going down!

I'm dropping jewels
So if you see sun (son) shine
You know who picked up my charm

Smile cause love warm and it lasts long
And hate just bring out the angry face
High blood pressure while they press on

I'm throwing alley - oops

So I let it glide in the air
Until you meet me there

Cause on this team
If you fall?
We all lose

And I like winning

Brimming with teeth shining and dimples
That you could go deep sea diving in

I'm throwing Alley - Oops

I wink my eye
So that you know
That I know
We're on the same page
That's to score with ease

I'm throwing Alley - Oops

For every kid who was told
They ain't good enough
But only ever needed a push in the right direction

Play like you matter

I'm throwing Alley - Oops
To get you off your seat and cheer

Because we made it, hot in here
We brought windmills, to you cool off

I'm throwing half court
No look passes
Jason Kidd but I ain't kidding around

I'm throwing Alley - Oops

Because you worked hard and held on to hope and faith

That your time would come

So this that miracle

Falling out of the sky

I'm throwing Alley - Oops

What are Those?

What are Those?

Those are the new blood, sweat and tears
Those are Sacrifice

Those are the blues sung like a harmony

Those are old but clean
(I got 10s but I'm a keep em clean though)

Those are tailor made
Part hustle and part struggle

Those are what I like
And if you don't
Stop looking
Who are you anyway, the fashion police?

Those are the shoes I use to walk away from you who
Spend their last
Just so
They won't laugh

That try so desperately to be in the inner circle
Of a room full of squares

Those are out of the box
Far away from what you know
The status quo

Those are Nunya
Nunya?
None ya business

Those are the shoes that will make a thousand miles
(Well they look like you put a thousand miles in them already!)
Shut your mouth!

You know what?
Since you want to be a smart ass
Those are the shoes I use to kick your ass!
Those are the trendsetters
Hot steppers*
(Here comes the hot stepper, murdera!)

Those are boots, running shoes and walkers
Through
Rain, sleet, hail, snow

Those are the sew according to my means
Those are so comfortable
You could fall asleep, standing

Those are my baller sneaks
Those are called hard work
Determination
Those are confidence
Those are built to last
Those are respect
So you can't tell me nothing
Those are what I got
Those are the new

Heir(Air)... To the Thrones

Coming soon......
At a sneaker store near you
(Restrictions may apply see void where prohibited)

Mind and Matter

Times like these I fall in love with myself

I was in the back on the shelf
At the back of the bus
Nobody counted on me
Nobody thought about us

It was just me

With a rhyme, pen and a pad
Thinking I was nice

They didn't think I had somewhere to be
Didn't think I had somewhere to go

They didn't think I had a voice
My shit was slit from the throat

But I came like a ghost
Into myself

Reinvented myself

Cause I figure if we gonna die
We gonna live first

We ain't going out like that

You see this here time is of the essence
We realize time can be taken just like that
And we take it for granted just like that

So I said just like that I'm gonna flash forward

I'm gonna take my fear and make a style out of it
We gon call it a
Spoken Word Poet and I'm gonna know it

And if I don't know it
You gon act like I know it cause damn it how many times didn't I
know it?

How many times was I sssecond guessing myself?
Ssscared!?

So I said there I go
Putting belief in myself they confused it as arrogance
I said there I blow
Call it a fault but I'm there arrogant

There, I know

I turned it around cause I studied myself

Here's the hoax
We learn everything about everybody else
But we forget about ourself

Study
Look yourself in the mirror and study because you are just as
important and valuable

I know celebrities make us feel cool
Everybody wants to be that
It's cool, ok

You want to be on TV
I don't have no hate on you

But you are just as important too
Don't forget about yourself

Cause sometimes life will erase that chapter and we will be missing
in its pages
Too many blanks

They became history
We wanted to be just like them
But we forgot we were just as
Great

I'm tired of being overlooked and overshadowed
So my name is Emilio The Poet and you gonna know it
Even if I gotta tattoo it in your cerebral

Mind over matter
If you don't mind, it don't matter

But I'm gonna make you mind and matter

It was Supposed to be Summertime

It was supposed to be summertime
We were supposed to have fun
It was supposed to be Summertime
It was just a grocery store

I mean c'mon.....we kids!

I mean I want candy and I'm a grown ass man
It's supposed to be Summertime

We just kids man
How much fun it is to grab yourself an Icey
Yea I know it's night time
I should've been asleep

But we all sneak, creep
15!

You supposed to be touching my heart

I'm not supposed to be bleeding through my veins

We just kids!

I mean if you don't like me?
You might punch me but that's that!

And that's already too much
In fact where's the knife in that?

I mean if you don't like me?
Sleep me*
But that's that

But we live
We supposed to be kids

This is summertime
What am I doing dead?
Street corner where I was supposed to be playing hide and seek
I'm just a kid!
This is summertime!
Where's the fun in these times?

I don't give a shit what's going on
We was cooped up for eight months!
Winter had it going strong

I was supposed to go outside
Just to free my mind

For a knife to hit my neck, back, spine?
I'm dying?
Why!?

They say Justice for Junior
I say Justice for every child on earth

Cause what happened was bullshit!

If you an older, brother, sister are a parent
Get in your kids ear
Cause when we don't do that

We killed him too!

Hip Hop Stole My Tongue

I know it was Hip Hop
I know it was

Cause the last thing I recall was loud thumping sounds from
speakers
Where back seats use to be

Came like a ghost in the night and stole my heart and pierced my
identity

I swear I had it here a minute ago

In the corner of White Plains Road and Morris Park

Where head nods replaced direct commands of stand still

And a slight limp
Replaced upright walks
With a slight drop of the pants by the waist

Where it's music was our companionship

There was no need for Headphones because loud thumping sounds
from speakers where back seats use to be
Held us down

Hip Hop crept up and got in between my pages of
Psychology, Philosophy and the Autobiography of Malcolm X

Forcing this huge inevitable rap battle between
Being formal and street slang terminology

The outcome?
Intellectual Dopeness

The marriage between books and street
Where walking, had a new rhythm

And the world could only see
As headphones handcuffed my brain and allowed my heart to beat in
unison with

Hip Hop

New York

New York
Where space is limited
Where narrow roads meets the United Nations
of Cultures

On one block

The melting pot
You done seen it all

They say, if you can make it here
You can make it anywhere

And that goes for driving too

Subways remind you that

There may be a tad, too many people in this great city

It's nitty gritty, dirty and clean all on the same street

Homeless reeks
Welcome your front row seat
Next to the lady with all her children and them bad ass kids that
won't sit still
Shits real

Where
Either you are an aggressive driver or you get run over

Where patience is like an alien

We've all heard of it but never seen the shit

New, York
Cause we're trend setters and if ain't here

It doesn't exist
You won't find it

So don't bother looking for it

Where the world is at your feet
So there's no need to travel to it

It finds you in every street corner
Attached to a bodega
Where a dollar can take you real far in life!

Where a whole city is accessible
With one metro card swipe

Where we have more bridges and tolls then we know
What to do with!

Where good parking is like hitting the lotto
We get excited as shit!

Where ignoring people is our space because personal space is a
luxury nobody can afford

Where you can't escape rush hour

It's gonna get you one way or another
Like the IR.S
Yes you feel the stress from too much work and not enough pay
Where the whole city exhales, simultaneously on the train

Rushing like their being chased by mandatory overtime with no
compensation

Where you look like a punk for taking lunch

Where you are supposed to work but no fun

From early mornings A.M.'s

Just do it all over again, tomorrow

New York

Let Them Know

Let them know that we were here

Let them know that we were here and that our ears were the warm
shoulders your words needed to cry on

Our look was all the attention you needed to feel beautiful

Our smile was the cool spring breeze
Followed by the sweet caress of the sun's fingertips at your face

Our dimples the depth of our love

Let them know them our hearts could not be contained in no chest
because then that would make its walls selfish and these walls ain't
no damn prison

That our passion was the childlike excitement that adulthood could
never hold a candle to and those who deem us immature we say
Pleeeewww! To you

Let them know that we took all of our emotions
Fear, Love, Hate and turned it into a style and left everyone a
roadmap

Marked our trails in red, so you could follow in our footsteps

Let them know that in a world where masks of pride did a great job
to disguise we walked naked
Baring it all because they say you can't take anything when you are
gone
So we took that saying figuratively

Let them know that our mouths spit seeds to be planted onto
incoming brains

To grow love, compassion, progress, destress and life

Let them know that we were walking dart boards, the first line of defense

We took the bullets of shame, fear and scorn and met it with a forcefield of triumph and poetic tears

Let them know that we smiled so big that our faces hurt and we took pain and made books, verses and films out of them

Just let them know that we were magicians because we took bullshit and turned it into sugar

*That when the world gave us hell
We were too busy staring at rainbows trying like hell not to waver from that pot of gold*

All the while leaving footprints on their souls

Let them know that our kindest was a staircase made to elevate

*Not a floor mat for you to step all over and clean your feat but just in case you thought it was
We pulled the rug right from underneath you*

Let them know that life was not to blame for they didn't know our greatness

Yet

Let Them Know

To My Unborn

If you ever get afraid get very excited
Because the other side of that is living!

Breath deep and consume the present moment
Because right now there is nothing more important
Don't talk with your mouth full

Unless you like complete strangers giving you mouth to mouth!

Don't be so hard on yourself
Instead learn to love you and all of your imperfections
Master your strengths and work on your weaknesses

Be your own number one fan!
Supporter, admirer

Pat yourself on the back
So you can leave hand prints for others to know where they can
leave there's at!

Lead with enthusiasm
In everything you do!
On the road less traveled, back up, U-turn and drive in circles if you
have too
Be wise but not a wise ass

Take a chance
A shot
Not with a gun

Unless you really have too
But save violence for last

Instead keep a full clip in your mouth of intellect

Be well spoken, proper

Always have something interesting to say
But listen way more than you speak

So read
Books and people

Listen like people's words are your life line
Because the fastest way to clear a room is to turn your conversation
into a speech

Cause nobody paid to hear you
Loving the sound of your own voice

Do good even when nobody's looking

Keep an open mind
And don't be afraid to speak yours

And if your gonna stand alone
Stand up straight and keep your head high
Do it with pride

And make it so the side walk your standing on is a goldmine
So fine that people want to push you out of the way
Just to take your place

When it comes to your inner peace
Play good D

That means guard it like crazy!

Value yourself
Know what you bring to the table

Pray with all of your might!

Not because you are religious but because you have faith in better
and you believe with your soul that it is possible
Be grateful

Show your appreciation

And tell people exactly how they make you feel

Smile, even if people think you're crazy
But smile because that's the beginnings of being happy
Be humble

But in the jungle be a lion
Work your tail off while others are lying
On their backs

Dress with confidence
And surround yourself with upbeat, supportive, positive people

Speak up and say it with your chest!

Defend yourself with the gift of gab and let slabs of facts be your
main ingredient

Know that life is a culmination of moments
And there are miracles and blessings wrapped within fragments of
turmoil and torment
And the faster you can accept it, the faster you can curb depression

Learn Spanish
Because your Father speaks it
Plus it traces you back to your roots and you get to be in two
cultures simultaneously

And that's....cool

Be aware of people and your surroundings
Never trust blindly

Keep a stash of optimism in your shoebox for humanity

Know there will be ups and downs
Shine anyway

Get on your purpose
If you don't know what your purpose is
Be patient with yourself and others and stick to the things you enjoy most

Put your best foot forward, on the pedal to success
Top speed

And if you can't do that
Aim to do better than your best

Be unselfish

Be in love even though your heart was melting
Because in the end you are right
And there's no greater feeling than loving and being loved!

Impact others in ways, they could only ever imagine

And if you chew like a horse
Take your ass to the local barn and stay ya ass their!

Keep an open mind
Try new things
Hug with your heart because sometimes that's all a person really needs

And always remember
That I

LOVE YOU

ABOUT THE AUTHOR

Emilio Montilla has been writing since the age of 16 and been an Educator for over a decade. Yet no matter what he's done writing and performing has always pulled at him like a magnetic force. He's been an Amateur at the show Amateur Night at the Apollo in Harlem, New York. Has performed on off Broadway Productions such as: A Sketch of New York written by Joe DiNozzi and Darien Di Maria, Sing for the Lonely Planet and Sure Thing written by Ted Talk Speaker, Eunice Hudak. Emilio has also been featured on several television series' such as: Law and Order SVU, Blue Bloods, Blacklist and Orange is the New Black.

You can contact the author on Instagram @emilio_thepoet
OR
Via Email: Emiliothepoet@gmail.com

94075136R00076

Made in the USA
Middletown, DE
17 October 2018